It Broke Anyway

April Michelle Bratten

NeoPoiesis Press, LLC

NeoPoiesis Press

Inquiries:
P.O. Box 38037
Houston, TX 77238-8037

Primary Address:
2775 Harbor Ave SW, Suite D
Seattle, WA 98126-2138

www.neopoiesispress.com

Copyright © 2012 by April Michelle Bratten

All rights reserved. No part of this book may be used or reproduced in any manner whatsoever without express written permission from the publisher except in the case of brief quotations embodied in critical articles and reviews.

April Michelle Bratten – It Broke Anyway
ISBN 978-0-9855577-6-8 (paperback : alk. paper)
    1. Poetry. I. Bratten, April Michelle

Printed in the United States of America.

First Edition

for Jane Mullins Bratten

Contents

Like Ekmek, with Dirty Hands 1
The Wedding 3
The Man of Dark 4
Traveler 6
The See-Through Girl 8
In this Field 10
Eat My Paper 11
I Was Born Next to a Trolley Car 12
Strong Jane 13
The Blind Woman 14
a disobedience 15
Antlers 16
No Roses 17
Twenty-five 18
Stealthy Walks with Granny 20
Fell 21
3 Horses 22
June 26th, With Too Much Water 24
Daylight Saving 26
In the Dry of My Turkish 28
I Am Not a Horseback Rider 32
Boxing the Fat 34
Asleep on Magazine Street 38
Whistling 39
The Open Mouths of Fish 40
First Kiss 42
Switch of Lightning Beat 43
American Swagger 44
The Catch 45
I am as clear as a raw egg-white 46
Legs 50
rest/stop 51
Barracuda Mommy 52
Balls 54
Kaleidoscope 55

The Blood Memory	56
all the little feet	58
Blood Salt Tang	60
Kitchens	61
An Early Vision of Ponthipa	62
My Mouth Has Turned Graveyard	63
Orange	64
Big Things	65
Especially When God Turned His Head	66
Signals	68
He Likes When I Wear Skirts	69
The Professional	70
Death Mark	71
The Rabbit	72
To Hurricane Juan, 1985	73
The snow jar	74
Baumkuchen	75
Forever 19	76
She Moves As I Move	77
Last Song for Minot	78
Invisible Night	79
Waterless	80
Machine	81
Long Bones	82
Neighbors	83
Off the Highway	84
Air Bright	85
Say Hello to No	86
A Devil Says to Me	88
I Found God While Watching Frank Wash the Dishes	90
Pacifist Afternoon	92
The Quiet Room	93
The Threat	94
Choking on the Rope	95
That Breakfast in Savannah	98
That Dinner in Savannah	100
Where Does the Light Go?	101
Never Swallowed the Kamikaze	102
Highway 83 North, 3 a.m.	103
The Lost Story of Mary	104
greater than	106

Heights	107
The Bottle Tree	108
Circles	109
The Last Whale Song in the Badlands	110
the hand job	111
I died with it all so easily	112
Don't Go, Janie	114
A Red Horse	115
Papers	116
Modern Owls	118
the church door	119
Mersin	120
Happy Joe	122
The Determined Undermining of Summer	123
It always burns a little when it goes in	124
Up the Whiskey Tree	125
A Telescope and Other Instruments of Persuasion	126
Skin	130
The Bird	132
Scavenger	133
Letters	134
It Will Only Hold For So Long	135
Marriage	136
In the Neighborhood	138
No Gentle Thing	139
Never Cross	140
Impressions	142
Worth in Silver	144
This is My Favorite Sky	146
International Gothic	147
4th of July	148
What Horace Remembers	149
Lid on Tight	150
It Broke Anyway	151
For the Girl I Have Named Tonic	154
Nipping at Heels	156
Warmth	157
I Thought of Stars	158
Professor Zitelli's Tiny Chai Glass	159
Thick	160
This is the Earth	162

Stop 163
Can You Smell That Too? 164
The moon isn't the only lonesome thing 166

Like Ekmek, with Dirty Hands

I was as clear as her rows of shining glass,
tall bottles stashed under her sink.
I remember the day my name became Vodka
in another country,
how she dared me to grip the bottle
with little pale fists,
and I knew I would collapse and crawl inside
the damage of a thirst.

I was still fresh then,
grown from the fronts of planes
and the backs of cars.
I had never heard the sweeping of a different
kind of gunfire,
had never heard the rage of a woman banging
her fists against cement floors.

I thought myself noble,
crunching snails with my bare feet,
holding geckos in the sunburn of my palm,
letting them roast in the deadly of my heat.

I miss Gul's hair,
the way her mouth formed my name
on a hardened tongue.
I used to watch her read backwards from books,
her fat nose was a brown weapon,
and her covered legs, a chai wonder.

I would wake to touch the bells of her yard,
sing, "Gul, Gul, Gul!"
until her head sprouted from the other side of the wall,
pinked, and
I would wonder where her tenacity came from,
the ability to hold the man, without want,
obligation piling her tough skin.

She was like a mother and I dreamed
of her placenta with me nestled inside,
but she squatted over holes,
and took the back handed slap
of men, men, men.

She smelled of grease and tomatoes,
and when language failed us,
we would just smile,
teeth showing,
gnawing at the differences of choice and chance.

White girl,
she does not remember you!
Her paper napkins are collecting themselves
on a shelf somewhere she used to call home.

I hide my crosses,
bury my peaches inside the dried up earth,
because I was born from the desert instead,
where water only comes from bottles
and milk from boxes.

I still live for the hope of water,
but when my organs shrink down to their exactness,
I will be savagely torn from the whole,
like ekmek,
with dirty hands.

The Wedding

The leaves opened their mouths wide
and yelled through the branches like animals.

I could not hear your words
over the moaning of nature,

but my throat crunched up anyway
at the simple spider that climbed your dress
and the slight shaking I saw in your shoulders

and him
smiling at me from a folding chair
as he drank a beer.

I still do not know exactly what love is
and perhaps I never will

as the promise of family has now taken
a different shape,

but the concept grew a little more clear that night
as we held hands in the dark wind

and ran through the yard, laughing

when the fireworks created new stars
that blasted louder and more beautiful

than any sorrow of trees.

The Man of Dark

I

She liked to touch his handcrafted leather purses,
his scratched albums,
the unfinished sketches and paintings
that he would never finish,
half-moons, one quarter horse heads,
one third phantoms of women he forgot to love.

While he was out, kissing strange girls
in jazz clubs,
Gail would pretend to float on her back.
She imagined herself beautiful,
a crying blonde, or a temptress, sparkling red,
in one of Joe's paintings.

She would watch her body turn blue and glowing,
a night train from his bed.
She could be an angel
or a ballerina,
as she practiced en pointe,
flexing and pointing her little feet
toward the edge of his covers.
Her tiny fingers dotted the shift of night
like white stars.

She would point and stretch,
excited by the dark and the twinkle
that caught against her white belly.

II

One night in the attic,
as Gail floated thick as a fish,
a man of Dark appeared before her.
He was blacker then Joe's walls,

blacker than the tar or oil on their driveway,
blacker than the blackest of all the black nights.

He did not glow like she did.

As she froze in mid-horizontal-pirouette
the man slid his crow hand out
toward her stunned face,
but he did not touch.
He kept back an inch or two,
a paperweight to hold Gail's chest from moving.

III

They stayed like that all night,
Gail's mouth open in still song,
the man of Dark, pointing into it,
until the sun drowsily climbed the edges
of the walls.

The man turned to dust in light,
and Gail regained movement
in her paralyzed limbs.

She crept, quite flat footed now,
down the steps into her mother's kitchen.
She stood in the doorway,
a trembling strip of bacon on a griddle.

Janie just shook her paper,
flicked her cigarette,
and peered at Gail over the sharp rim
of her brown reading glasses.

She shook her head, said,
"Yeah, darlin'.
That was the Reaper comin' for Joe."

Traveler

My homes had each been slaughtered,
colored red or orange by the lights of Virginia
where God knew the length of my limbs,
my oak-dressed soul,
and the dusk that settled over the rum-soaked townhouse

and Louisiana, South Carolina,
I remember your curtains,
brown and stiff, with no banjo, no guitar
to lean against the dust cluttered windows,
no books along the floor,
only thin Mother inside your doors with pale broom

and sister Tennessee,
with its different southern sun of lashes shutting,
re-opening to rain, oil, bridges, and she,
lonely on a porch talking,
black hair dipped in cheap sweet wine
attracting those fruit flies

no matter,
what is it now,
damp barn of North Dakota,
sling-temple of dirt and plain,
a square piece bright and stout,
where he and I took photographs once in that knee-high grass,
we, the trespassers,
to fade our country one state at a time

and over the straight sight of the middle-west
we fell into our own attachments,
some might even call it love,
with the watchful eye of Father
and the degenerate's passion
over dry Missouri,
over dry Kansas in late May

where the road created a house out of its yellow lines
and smooth pavement,
where dead musicians and dead poets painted us,
round and slightly toxic,
and you became pointed, poignant,
with arms above your body,
our own pocket full of roof.

The See-Through Girl

The first time Kyle punched me,
he did it on the thigh.

He said he imagined
bashing my head in
with a hammer
on a quiet evening
in the summer.

I asked him then,
what is the point
of banging
through a ghost?

He kept trying
to kill me anyway,
usually on
Saturday nights,
after the booze ran
lukewarm and thin,
the music sputtered
and dulled out,
and his boiling eyes
caught me red-cunted,
turned me translucent.

He did it because his socks weren't sparkling white.
He did it because I had the mean face of a fish.
He did it because he simply ran out of things to say.
He did it because he felt like it.
He did it again and again until his hands unscrewed
and returned to feathers.

The last time Kyle punched me,
the ghost left the house.

I followed her,
that see-through girl,

all over town
until she stopped
by the woods
and held out a hand
full of leaves.

She was blue,
or maybe it was just the sky
behind her,
but she was there
and she was grinning
like a goon.

In this Field

I am the broken barn
that sits, a child,
cross-legged,
on the side of the highway.

In the winter I wait,
my roof checked black
and perked with snow.

I would rather be the haystack,
tightly wound and warm,
rolling my haunches
by a bright patch of sunflower.

My hair would be the smell of earth,
and I would be happy and round,
naked and full.

I am only a wish,
blown from the seeds of the dying dandelion,
and from down here I see
there are no trees on the prairie,

only a North Dakotan sky,
her blue, carried in a hand-basket,
tinged with white.

She never serves a day without the sun,
a constant head of orange that sometimes warms,
that gentle light inside the piercing cold.

The wind, how she pushes
the rights and lefts of me, all of me.

Oh, wind,
you are a greedy mother,
and you have kept me here
in this field.

Eat My Paper

I scatter landmine pieces of paper
around my bedroom.
They have scribbled secrets
across their white backs.
Receipts, fliers, napkins,
and bits of jealousy.
Paper sticks to my walls
and screams down from the ceiling,
but lately, I have noticed,
they have started disappearing.
I saw once,
when you thought you were alone,
how you stuffed one in your mouth
like a packet of sugar.
You eat my words
when no one else is looking.
You let them swim deep inside your belly,
just to have a piece of me
that is a rampant animal,
tightening around your cock.

I Was Born Next to a Trolley Car

I was born
next to a trolley car
in the deep south.

The air weighted itself
on my mother's chest
as she stretched
out on the ground,
an ugly angel to split,

her bare feet
spread and burning
on hot concrete and
dry whistling weeds.

She wore a blue pinafore
which she held up
with two gripping hands
as a scream
ripped through her body,
an iron wedge of sound.

The sun was just nodding its head,
owning the sky,
a blunt rock of angry light.

There was a groaning,
a sickness in the grass,
a wide open smell.

The trolley car just rang its bell
and pulled away from us,
leaving me naked,
and her,
fat and bleeding.

Strong Jane

My grandmother used to shave her legs dry
in the front yard with an old rusty
disposable razor.

Her worn skin would flake off
with the prickles of hair,
leaving behind an old tire in the grass.

"My skin ain't soft, no way,"
she would say, bent over the age of her legs,
the scrape of the blade flirting
with her cuts and bruises.

I would watch the swallow of her back
and see her far hills in Kentucky,
where no gold flushed sturdy
the hands of the family's mining saints.

She was the first to leave
when the call of sailors swept the winds
of that crowded shack,
and at 14,
she ran toward the sound of wind chimes,
and the sands of hours away from home.

On the shore she met a man in a beret,
and with him
she began to grow her bones like broomsticks,
her hairs like tough rubber.

The Blind Woman

for Eva Braun

Your time was told
 in collected teeth,
14 years of suns and moons
that only appeared
to rape the sky
with smiles of terrified light.

Their round shapes jutted out,
fearful, dead.

You embraced the power
of all the sad planets,
captured your own peace
next to the water,
your body open
and flipped back like a bridge.

Wie Shade!
Wie Shade!

The sky still keeps its blue on the hip.
Let it forever reject you.

a disobedience

I had a husband who used to hang like
Christ on a clothesline, an upside
down beggar of instinct, the pathetic
phoenix of only dust and limp prayers.

He would sleep on a communal cot of age,
demanding the falling of faces and hair,
his hands and feet, in bandages, in rot,
in the dilapidated sickness of hunchback.

I began to pin up his creeping shoulders,
stringed up messy with my foul wash,
to dry out the dampened feet of the fishwife,
the sinking heels of always more, never less.

His hands would flail at stubborn side,
to pull at apron hem, bonnet end,
tired knee, my dog love, like the careful
placement of cup in cup, fork on curve of spoon.

Antlers

Each morning my head turns
in great absurdity,
my feet crunching
an early path beneath my chair.

I have antlers,
antlers that bow over my table,
obscene protrusions,
dark and magnificent.

I sit strangely,
a boiling kiln above my head.

I am like you,
human,
but without bombs,
without explosions

to devastate,
or harass
those slippery hillsides.

My antlers glean,
spidering against the sky,
as others still,
with white hands creeping,

hang portraits from strings,
bits of origami to decorate me.

I will not become picturesque
or tame,
because in this moment,
I remain,
wanting.

No Roses

The people move like a conveyor belt of unintentional roses
over continents I will never see

they color the cities with their blood, they tame their primal urges,
they seek human kindness, they seek water

they blend together

In this pail, in this basket, in this trough, I find my own needs
like a tree that stands alone, current, yet unlinked,
horned flesh, barked, deeply veined, something like a human,

a failed monster of easy mornings, eggs, bacon, toast,
one tight chair, one stern table, one empty vase,

no roses, no roses.

Twenty-five

I drag my years behind me in a hollowed out melon,
the heavy heads of so many ages rolling,
plunking the green walls.
I yank them through bloodied grass and the empty of streets,
try to disturb their perfect sleep,
get them to cry out for me,
but their mouths have blackened and grown useless.

Twenty-five, with her eyes
like big dumb eggshells,
peers at me blankly from the edge of the rind.
I want to squeeze the reasons from her throat,
make her explain why, at 25,
I dug my fingers inside my own chest, and began to eat.

I was not a clean fruit to pick.
I was made bitter by the larcenist's hands
and his pocket sucker-fish mouth that attached to me,
nursed from me,
oh, crooked barb.

I can be a woman,
I can give him back to Twenty-five,
pry his bastard tongue from my hips,
and I will be clear tonight,
sinking myself from him like a 26 year old virgin.

Let him call my name loud as a scrape.
Let him lick tacky at my wounds,
because, no matter,
I still know that blood fills every yard that I struggle through,
and I know that circumstance grows rough along the roots of trees.

I am just a straggler, a hauler of collapsed years,
I am not known by any real name.
I can offer no mountains, give no hills.
My height is parallel to the flat inner thigh of nature,

but my mind is a warm plateau that will keep you,
riveted,
burning in your lap.
My ripeness is felt on the tongue,
and my storm burns fierce and quick.

Stealthy Walks with Granny

On warm nights
she and I
would wait until dusk
to steal into
the neighbor's yard
and secretly pick from their bushes
of blackberry.

We would stand
quietly,
she and I,
and wait for the sun
to slide down the hill
like a sleeping baby.

As the light waned,
we would shovel the berries,
black and red,
inside our pert mouths,
and they would explode,
little bursts of hurricane.

Then we'd smile,
our teeth purple.

Fell

The red park bench
pecked at my marriage
like a rooster,
hungry for some cracked corn,
or worms,
or whatever it is
that roosters eat.

Autumn made a bed
out of the park air,
became intimate
with the yellow chill,
the yellow trees,
the thin yellow oxygen.

It was there,
in a different color,
where I found myself
six months away from you,
my knees muddy in the golden earth,
my hands alive in the dead grass,

trying to see
how big
the gosling had grown
since last June.

3 Horses

The virgin mouths
of North Dakota
have never closed
around the sweet salt
of a sea bass,
have never attempted
to swallow the entirety
of a wheat field,
or caught the colors
frothy and quick,
on the tips of their tongues.

I have seen these mouths
crying in the streets,
have witnessed flowers
engulf the heads
of happy women,
clouds afflict the thoughts
of tired men,
have watched smoke blow
sorrowfully from the middle
of the people-less plain.

I have heard the songs
of abandoned instruments,
lonely highways,
and green empty graveyards.

I have touched new love
on the cusp of solitude
with a tender whipping-like
horse hair,
horses 3,
horses running in the streets,
horses strong,
unnamed and forgotten,
horses black,
horses white,

horses free and determined
like bodies on velvet,
horses hungry,
cold,
wet,
but never faithless,
never homeless,
horses with blood together,
2 sisters and brother,
love, love,
running in the streets.

June 26th, With Too Much Water

Pray, they say,
pray.

Accept what is holy.

I remain safe on the hillside,
tend to my paper flowers,
flimsy, unreal, without God,
and earnest without water.

My city,
70 percent underwater,
is dying.

I cannot pray.

I think about all the daughters
who remember their fathers
caring for the real growing thing,

a severe stem among dozens,
a piece of green and bright
mixed with all those other colors,

colors, colors.

Those daughters,
they are displaced
as I shower,
re-adjust my bra-strap,
and fit into a fresh pair of blue panties.

I cry,
but not enough,

as the water reaches new levels
and all the Daddies

pray

for a bit of grass to stretch
out from under
the flood.

Daylight Saving

Big-winged ladies,
tall as towers,
stomachs made of clocks,
point their long fingers,
scratch at their legs,
thunder their hair,
and position themselves
on my rooftop.

They say they are
the new American angels
brought here to teach us
about the vanishing of time.

They say they were sent
from out of the dark
just to stir our big pots of guilt.

Those clocks embedded in their bodies,
those damned clocks,
keep on tickin' in my ear,

and the ladies tick-tick-tick their heads with the sound,
twitch their mouths with the sound.

When I watch those ladies
with their beat-beat-beat,
I become enveloped
in the green of the streets,
swallowed
by a green protruding light,
my skin,
my own eyes,
all, now green,

as green as that barefoot grass
I went screaming into at 2 a.m.,
my sobs echoing off that terrible house,

as green as your eyes used to be,
as green as the love I used to feel for you.

Now the clocks in those horrible bellies grow bigger,
tick louder.

I can hear them better
than your miserable heartbeat.

I can hear them better
than all of those fighting ghosts,
can't you hear it now?

Tick, tick, tick.

In the Dry of My Turkish

Babies lie down
in the dry of my Turkish,
they do, they say,
they carry small pieces of bread
in a ringed hat.

They tell me when my smoke burns too thin.
They tell me when I try to create a life I cannot live
with parched lips and an empty glass.

I was once one of them,
the white chalk of an apple core,
but I have turned, a tricky grenade,
with romance hands on my back,
and only one hundred words to remember.

I have danced along the peaceful
rims of walls,
avoided all responsibility for love,

love,
that dried fat womb.

I will never be soft,
never compliant enough
to feel the sun rise in my chest,
a full, perfect circle.

I have burnt, a tough crusted shell
with too many indentations
upon the leg to raise it,
but you cry, you cry,
with the sounds of a terrible baby.

My body is left behind,
a wretched salt lick,
starved,

the silver that wraps your left ring finger,
a love like no other,
one I can never remove.

Sins bolt from my hips
because I'm the type of girl
who washes her feet in sand,
and shrouds herself
in the Middle Eastern touch.

I am one with the veil
and the cracked feet.

I am one with the cemented walls
and the sheepherders.

I won't see you here,
born and swaddled,
because I am a piece of dust
that flies from the camel's back,
or that small space of wall that climbs
from the neck of the great Mosque.

My legs still trudge the dirt like a mother,
but it's not the same.

I still look for the Suckler
that peeks from behind stained glass,
or that glass-less window,
the hole in the faded rock
that she used to wail my name through.

I keep watch for the Child
that kept a brilliant watch over me,
with her full lips and splendid brown eyes.

She was the answer to my solid straight hand.

100 Breezes

They said at first she didn't want to go,
that her husband made her
when he saw the pools of blood,
red and empty,
eye sockets on the bathroom floor.

She was vomiting the stuff everywhere,
the life leaving her eyes quickly
like a pissed off lover.

She must have been afraid,
terrified,
as she clutched a plastic bag in the truck
on the way to the hospital
and filled it with more blood from her shaking mouth.

She probably watched the night
flying by the window
and saw the way it appeared to swallow,
with a noisy gulp,
the entire southern shore.

They say she uses a walker now,
that her speech is slowed and slurred,
and that the doctor can no longer repair

the holes she created in her own stomach.

My grandfather sighed
when he spoke of her on Friday,
called her his "sweet-sweet girl,"

and I remembered how she used to be,
with cold beers on the beach,
sneaking me a wine cooler when I was 13,
how she loved the color purple,
Chinese food,
sweet wine in the box,

birds,
fast cars,
and pills.

I remember the tan on her small
but strong legs,

the sandals and tiny bikini she would wear
as she stepped forcefully on the clutch.

I remember how excited she was
that one evening
as she pulled out old newspaper clippings,
black and white photographs,
talked about ghosts,

and the strange shape of our noses.

I remember her fingernails,
and how they looked just like her mother's
as she poured herself another glass,

her eyes dancing
with the 100 breezes
of rolled down windows on the highway.

I Am Not a Horseback Rider

I am not terrified of horses.

I allow them in as chocolate pieces,
sticking in a sweet hoof to suck,
tenderly.

My mouth was made for it.

They run in circles all around me,
changing my femininity
into a slippery water slide,
but I am not a horseback rider,
only a sucker of wine and sweet cruelty.

I have begged for eyes,
I have begged for touch,
I have begged for ripping honesty to leave me
open and beautifully wounded,
my right hand striped with readiness.

These horses are too tender.
They sink into the mud with heavy meaty legs,
and I want to fully damage their falsities,
for no beast is as cunning as they.

Mighty nose,
smooth shank,
they could be powerful between my legs,
hurtful,
stretching and tearing at my soft insides,

but all horses fear the drive of a hesitant woman.

I used to be a stealer of horses,
walking them shameful,
crouched down
and leading them like a dead head of too many repulsive fires.

I have always wanted the lie,
to become equestrian,

but now their eyes know me like a ghost,
they wait for the tear at the mane,
the bite of the flank.

I love to leave my mark raised and round,
a patch work quilt across their name.

I will not fight this steed,
but burrow away inside of his cool stomach,
let him feed me how he chooses,
long grain, carrot, apple for my head,

but there is no more faith.

I am a million disasters,
each one ringing merciless over my head,
ready to crack me with their steady hammer.

I hold no brush to tame a disheveled face.
I am only an open ear,
a dry spout to place wet fingers within,
a sleepless woman on the back of an obstacle.

I am lived with, yet never broken.

Boxing the Fat

There is a room
where I like to keep them,
two circular ladies,
boxed up and contained
like a carton of mushrooms,
white and full,
round and
tasty.

I can hear them back there,
screeching their female
poetries, as they launch
their hefty back-sides
and fling their fertile arms
around that room,

thunks on the nightstand,
clatters on bookshelf,
knock of clothes hamper.

They hold shiny blue masks
up to their checkered faces.

Their mouths spill the beauties
of my impending death,
round and round
and round, "she's so washed up,
so wrung out,
I think she needs a wash, she's dying in."

Oh, these round cruel women,
they breathe out sun-made poems
from their meaty lips.

They spit the fat of their dresses
and roll lines of flowers between their thighs.

Sometimes I bring a chair

and sit outside their door
just to swelter inside
their pretty vernacular.

Oh, yes,
they are rotund,
singing perfect rhythms
from their wide lungs,
and I watch the roses curdle,
entwining the soft levels
of their supreme rib cages.

Sometimes I open that door
and let them shoot out
their dainty words,
prayers,
and then I watch
as those two monstrous bodies
rattle on the floor
like giant teething rings.

Wasting Tomatoes

I have grown soft in the kitchen.

I have let them stack around me,
great piles of tomatoes.

They line my counters like little bombs,
taunting me with big red toothy grins.

I have wanted to make sandwiches, stews.
I have wanted to gut them and take out their hearts,
strangle them of their juices,
hammer and smash them,
waste them into a nice pulp or paste
with a pound, pound, pound!

I do not.

I hold them in my hands, fragile things,
caress their red and ripe,
because a part of me still needs that juice
that holds, constricted in their skins.

There is no room in this kitchen for a thin soup
to slide down my arms,
to stain me red
with a love,
or a hate,
or some sort of vicious recycling,

but to betray them with a knife,
to slice them into quarters,
hollow them out,
and make thick muscular cages,

I will not.

I can dip them in grease, maybe,

let them harden and convulse,
allow little bits of meat to bird,
become trapped,
inside their fleshy walls of cage.

That grease will soon heavy,
swallowing those tomato cages right down,
until there is no more mushy and soft,

and they will bang the bottom of the boiling pot,
like rocks,

and I will be empty,
empty.

Asleep on Magazine Street

I slept hotly, burning on the hind legs
of Magazine Street.

The heat rioted my insides,
changed me, plated me,
a frazzled worm on the concrete.

I made that road my bed, sprawled out,
a white fan, I was shameless.

I waited for the slow cook of summer.

I cut the flowers away from their humid homes,
drizzled them over my chest like oils,
and while I slept,
I turned red and hard.

I awoke to find a caught dust
inside my palm,
an X on my skin,
tinted orange,
the ends pink.

I thought I had been killed.

There was no wind,
only the groan of the rusted stairwells.

I grieved with the lonely sound
as all the footsteps fell away,
and spring died in New Orleans.

Whistling

There is a sly whistling in the hallway.

It keeps on
like some insane trapped bird,

and each night,
I can hear my name
screeching out
from in between filthy teeth,
a hollowed mechanical music
of a dying animal.

It will not be consoled
with milk
or with water,
and it will not take the bread.

It just rattles in the hall,
its veins thrusting blue in persistence.

Tonight its volume
rises like a siren,
and it pecks and peels
at the broken wood of my door.

I stand on the other side,
an obscene object of light,
my arms a bridge,
and I will not let it enter

because another death inside this place
would flood my walls of their stone,
and take away the light.

The Open Mouths of Fish

He drops his sins
with bloodied fingers,
bouncing diamond notes
behind him.
He says
he wants to leave
something
for the wind.

When the days tire
and fold
onto the salted streets,
I can see him
dumping fish heads
from buckets,
planting
their skeletons
in the deep love
of his control.

When he is done,
he picks up his body
like a stumbling child,
and I follow
the walking sun
across the red bends
in his face.
I gather his eyes
into my hands,
feel the warmth of oysters,
salted and round.

He does not leave me
underwater
with the open mouths of fish,
but takes me

to the shattering

of cities,
where the buildings
line up
like rainbows
on the crusted edge
of the country.

We draw patterns
on their doors,
the familiar names
on graves,
and we find ourselves there,
tall stones above ground.

We can dance
with arms and legs
to the dirty beats
of home,
we can welcome
the flood
of one hand atop another.

First Kiss

Sloppily, immaturely,
in front of a pristine mirror
in the men's bathroom of my Baptist church,
I let that froggy-boy kiss me.

I remember the subtle
look of bewilderment in my eyes
as I clutched the wet sink
and allowed him to dive at me
with tongue and springy eye.

He did it without grace,
without the dented smell
of a flower in my pocket.

As he groped the front of my jeans,
I thought about that summer
Hurricane Hugo destroyed my family's
townhouse in Charleston.

We had to drag our belongings
through the grass and mud
to a new place,
smaller, ruder,
and somehow considerably more unstable.

Switch of Lightning Beat

There was a beast of mean grass,
a swatch of dirty green,
where I used to crouch
and write my swears and stories
on the tender belly of a battered tree.

That tree, my prickly umbrella,
supplied the instruments
that were used to fry and tar me.

I do not know why I would stay
long after the fiery hands of Mother
had made me a switch of lighting beat.

"Maybe the heat is just getting to me,"
I thought, as I waited there for the next slashing
with the dry white look of a saddled horse,
dumb revolutions shining, then dying,
like half-eaten freedoms in my eyes.

I can still hear her coming,
a miserable thing with a slither of sticks
to bounce off my bleeding back,
to choke more lines from my waiting skin.

American Swagger

With one last silver salute
from his spot-and-spiraled hand,
with all the dizzying sounds
of each airplane he ever saw
still rumbling in his chest,
he scrapes the foam from
his eyeballs and tilts his
mind toward a cold western sun.

His wife is from the south
and chestnuts crackle in her hair
as she pinches the desire for children
from her large round nipples,
and craves for her drops of milk
to fall inside two warm mouths
as black birds swoop and gather
in the new snow of an empty yard.

Silence was then
and is still now
a deep-fisted,
money-hungry memory,
a beard on a long last man,
a cloud that hovers gentle
next to the big mountain,
a liquor left warm and tight
overnight in a glass,
a sleeping child.

The straight line of a green plain
has become lost in their American swagger,
and now all they have known
has sharply turned into
glass particles, blood-sweat,
drowned in white.

The Catch

the bird stood
on one leg
in the rain

his little eyes
pinned to me

letting me know
he was on to me

and I wondered then
if he knew just how
similar
he and I really were

his head slashing
at the ground
for his desired prey

and when he rose
with a devil of a worm

a really bloody
fat worm
clutched protectively
in his beak

and turned his head back
to me
with a triumphant shake

I had no doubt.

I am as clear as a raw egg-white

Each summer I sweat an egg
that beats out like a heart.
It has rhythm.
It has Throb.
It can survive, but
without support,
it just waits to die,
to rot inside
of a great mouth of water.

It would prefer to die
inside of a delicate hand,
just as you,
just as I.

I must protect it.
I must keep the rhythm.
I must keep the Throb, or
the mosquitos will rise above it in volumes
to puncture,
hate,
and heave,
upon that gentle egg.

I do this honestly.
I do this passionately, but
each summer,
betrayal becomes the red
within the vile red
which I always carry.

I cannot refrain.
I poke a hole in the tender shell.
I suck-suck.
I drink from the egg which I had promised to protect.

In goes the slime,
slick, beautiful.

It makes me clear.
I am as clear as a raw egg-white.

History

History had a shame, a deep red shame
that turned rotten.

His scent shot up the air
with angry lightning bolts.

History was not handed to me
in a paper bag,
but I still ripped
and tore
and killed
and wheezed
and wanted
inside of it.

History held his hands out
in a persistent halt.

When I asked History to collect me,
take me under his breast,
and let me beat out like a wild woman,
he never let me.

I had the posture of a woman choking.

I say
his lies still fall like orphans
with heavy boots to dirty floors,
and I say, God, damn it,
History is a wire,
a dangling string
that connects me to an Unwanted.

I am done
allowing him to be
a useless god upon my chair,

his legs feeble,
spine curving his stupid neck of the dead.

When History grows old,
all things will leak.

He will hobble around
with a kerchief under his cock,
still searching for magic
and the feel of the fish-pull,
a hook tugging,
a silver spectacle of slice n' cut me.

He will never understand
the filthy prattle of life.

I have fucked in unoriginal places,
I have been pelted on the sides of houses,
with white paint clinging to my back-side.

I am a square of marble now.
I am centered,
and made of intelligible ingredients.

History can put his small palm up against me
and I will make a perfect angle,
never again to repeat,
never allowing his weight to crush on top.

Legs

I finally decided to shave my legs
somewhere outside of Baton Rouge,
just as your head (lookin' like a
rusted skillet) swung toward the road.
You rubbed your bear-like belly,
complained, complained,
of the hunger and the peas and rice.
I said what does it matter, I can't cook no-how.
The sun started spillin' just then,
poured smooth liquor over my calves.
I found a flat sharp stone to chisel
at the coarse hairs.
You pointed your toes toward the north.
I decided to make a bed right there,
on the side of the road, somewhere outside of Baton Rouge,
in the sparse grass, inside the weeds,
and small nippled-rocks.
You burned like a kerosene lamp on a hill.

rest/stop

While I clenched my teeth
under the comfort-eating moon,
frozen rain fell, rice
on the highway,
and his lips beside me
just kept smack-smacking
at my thin oxygen,
his body, red and irritable,
a terrible splotch
of human being
in the passenger seat
at 4 in the morning
somewhere in Eastern Montana,
and the road,
the car,
the wind,
the night,
all lurched across the countryside
like drunks in the dark,
while the coyote perched on the roof
of the rest-stop,
claiming that pit his own private mountain,
his prowling teeth clenched
and burning brightly
inside the black gums
of his proud mouth.

Barracuda Mommy

She was a mean fish, he said,
a walking, talking, up-right Barracuda,

but the length of her bite could reach
all of his starving sensitive places,
and he thrilled from the sexual noises her snout made
as she dropped him
and dragged him,
a man-sized corpse from her excessive ankles.

She limped from his weight
as he curved around her thick tree stump legs,
but she would continue to lumber
from one room to the next,
always with that man around her feet.

Her toes must have been dipped in sugar
to keep a man stuck like that,
his thirsty hands seizing her slick gray flesh.

If he really wanted to keep her,
he should have pinned a bell to her stubborn neck,
or leashed those stumps to the bed,
because her hoof-like feet were surprisingly nimble
and soft on the hardwood
once he tired,
and she would venture out without him
as he slept his dumb man's sleep.

She would leave to find the mother in her,
her womanhood,
as she wagged her pussy down each damp street
hoping her smell would bring Baby home.

Baby had been gone for years,
passed from mother to mother,
her little fat fists churning tunnels in softened eyes,
bleating out her noises with one shiny milk-tooth.

Baby suckled different fingers now.

That woman knew she was never really a mother,
but she never stopped looking,
hauling down those drinks,
wriggling down the city at night
to smother the echoes of those feverish church bells
that tolled so very loudly between her ears.

Balls

I know a thing or two
about balls.

There are men
who pretend to have them,
filling their little flaps with jelly.

There are men
who actually hate their own,
folding them in their laps like paper.

There are men
who will not leave them alone,
puffing,
feeling,
tugging
at skin and hair.

I tell them all,
it
is
just

flesh.

I once touched a set that was as rough
as sandpaper.

It confused me.

I thought all manhood was made to slide,
easy velvet,
down a woman's hardened skin.

Kaleidoscope

Age has crept over me.
I am a tired vessel of storm.

A smattering of rain
exits my bad throat
to spit out
all the places I have been.

They make a spinning map
in the air, a kaleidoscope
that I bend
and place my head into.

I let it breech me
with a swirling parade
of pint-sized hammers.

The lines of all the states
start bleeding their colors,
and the blending is
a sweet confusion
of names,
faces,
homes.

I can taste their ache
as they become
the great splash
that stains my skin.

The Blood Memory

In that womb-ish space,
happiness diffused
inside the blood balloon.

My tiny hands
felt it disappear
as they reached in vain
to grasp that retreating
rhythm muscle.

Boom-boom. Boom-boom.

I could hear
muffled foul words,
taste their static in rivulets
as they poured down
into my willing body.

This is a memory,
a stained one,
an elementary one
that could be spruced up
with other items in the scene:

thick books
with yellowed pages,

light summer dresses ruined by grass,

or a broken plate,
its pieces, white,
a contrast to all of that red,

but there was nothing but blood,
from top to bottom,
left to right--

some strains jellied

and curdled,
some pools watery,
loose,
dripped from the insides of the body.

I remember myself
flipped
like a pancake
inside my entrapment,
from one side to the other,
splash!

My heart was a tiny sliver of fire,
a thunder constrained.

My mother's scream escalated
to a higher pitch
that pounded my baby brain,

and my father's retaliation—
a tender flick on my wrist--

Blood-blood. Blood-blood.

all the little feet

i felt long and natural,
centered
on a vagrant star,
bent in mud
to accept rain
in all its forms:

static musical
against tin cans,
warm bubbling
on protective nets,
cool in the tree.

pitter-pitter-
patter!

"you can manage, you can manage, you can manage,"

as we trudged past
the fox
who dreamt of eating me,
the enemy
inside his stolen valley,
and from his watcher's cliff,
his head,
dark, fierce,
appeared in the mountain
to wink
in my general direction.

toward the clam bake creek,
I licked mud fish
and the borrowed hands
of travelers,

history all in a quick flow,
warm water over my blisters,

no fire in the dust,
or broken branch on the sweet death.

it takes us,
a toil in volcanic leftovers.

my poetry feels fine,
rumbling in the grass.

Blood Salt Tang

Show me your ugly, soft,
and deep tomato brain
that perches like a peacock
atop your skull.

Show me your feet and the little buds
that nestle their round asses
between your toes.

Show me your arms
and the loose cigarettes
that roll from your palm to elbow.

Show me your brass skeleton,
your scramble of veiny wires,
the sheep-head of your penis,
and let me milk it.

Let's go out into the country
where brown and green
mean the same thing.

Let's touch our many colors
under a bald sky,
flavorless moon,
and the peeking bland air.

Let's get to the point of things,
the beginning of things.

Let's wipe our heart pumps clean and dry,
and leave our chests open,
blazing bursts
of light and sweat and blood salt tang.

Kitchens

Feed the man. Feed him good.

Meat. Vegetables.

Solanum.

Body.

Body. Body.

It isn't crushed, it is not exasperated, the mind.
It is just the light, the light from the window,
playing devious, but puny tricks.
Food brought from kitchens, meals in the summer,
will not harm the hand, will not dismember the soul.

We wait for the hour to clear.
We wait and we wait.
Smoke emits from the kitchen.
It is only a grease fire.
Wait for it. Wait for it.

I create meals. He eats them with fervor.

Husband, wife.

Consume and be done with it.

Meat. Vegetables,

Solanum.

Never the body. Always the body.

Ripen.

Wait for the smell.

An Early Vision of Ponthipa

Her sex appeared in curious places--
underneath the elephant's feet,
in pools of the swallowing dirt,
stripped cruel and lovely
inside a make-shift Thailand,
a call in the gill of a fish
found cut and battered.

I wanted fingers like hers,
rice stained brown ponies
that pried the thin sheets apart,
made quick work of my tastes,
tripped the sounds of orchids,
found the staircases to my sadness,
and held my cries in their easy fold.

With each inevitable goodbye,
she could bend her wonton skins
to my devouring,
make herself tiny to fit, sizzling,
in the open wave of my mouth,
and I would jab my ugly fingers in
to touch the peaks
of her clear wrinkly film,
the crushed eggshells of her touch.

My Mouth Has Turned Graveyard

My mouth has turned graveyard,
as if death could carry me,
as if I could carry death,
as if I could crawl bare kneed
to save the sparrow.

I am not woman enough
to fall asleep near the wild onion root,
to carry a boy
inside my mother-parts,
to guide an attentive heart
around the sad curve
of flown pale eyes,
or to love the hand that finds my own.

I have found no solace for this
in lost languages,
and I do not wish to speak
of the ghost I know
who clings my legs,
or the warm tickle of little fingers
that pool the elbow.

Instead I heap beds of dirt
inside my womb
(good enough for no-thing
to rest a tired head)

to keep the worms hungry,
to keep the hair grown wild,
to keep the glass broken,
to keep the egg as my own,

to stomach the makers with
their loud beating wings.

Orange

I want to be vivid in the orange light of Turkey,
lie down in that country with curled warm flesh, pale orange,

around the orange skin of pumpkins, to bury my knees
in the foreign brown mud, my face alight in orange sun.

I want to wear the orange fabrics of Turkey,
an orange skirt over my orange knees, an orange headscarf

that I would wrap over my hair and eat sweet oranges
while sinking my feet into a pile of Turkish orange petals.

My fingers will be sticky with the juice of orange squash,
and my lips will taste of orange color, burnt and nectarous,

as I walk the streets lined with dark orange buildings, paint
myself, a woman in desperate shades of orange, along the walls.

I want to paper myself in orange napkins and kneel before
the little mosque outside of Incirlik, the orange glass

shining brightly orange in the glare of sun,
my skin finding its home in the sand, beautiful and orange.

Big Things

The silence is man and wife,
white on white.

We sit outside and realize that
grasshoppers use words bigger
than you and me.

Especially When God Turned His Head

for Stephanie

A tin roof
slick with rain,
the remnants
of floating life,
slipped from her hands,
a prayer mounted from
her chest
holy holy broken painting
of dim colors.

She allowed patience
to enter her sad mouth,
her private chapels
infiltrated by a clutter
of ravenous birds,
and those bibles
would not scatter
nor shake the shadows
fallen from her devotion-shaped
breaths.

She cried
like a Sunday night,
a secret
that filled the holes
in her walls and doors,
a secret
that filled the ropes
of her sorrow-filled womb
soft sinking
forgiveness
on the last sigh
of leaving wind.

The flowers brought
to her knees

were from his daddy's grave,
tied with a sob,
tied with two ribbons
a cry bouquet meant
for promises, meant
completely for love,
praise, home,
and the gentle
drying of spun clothing.

She found herself
in the crunch
of a lone concrete walkway,
in the peeling of foundation,
another perfect day
in the song of her mind,
where the sky would never burn,
or wear down her intimacies.

She is the bell broken,
and her flaw in glass
reflects no pointing angel
her lifting
and parting
of a skirt's hymn
was made entirely
out of paper.

Signals

It was deep into the crawl
of an early Wednesday morning

when you were tricked by my feign of sleep.

You crept in, touched my ankle
with your slightly destitute hands,
warm, buttery.

I listened to your bat signals,
creak, creak, creak.
I listened to your sounds
of leaving.

The
door
closed.

I watched from my bedroom window,
still fully dressed,
I watched from my bedroom window

as you walked slowly to your truck,
hesitated,
reluctantly hopped inside,
and touched your rear-view mirror,

as softly as you touched my left ankle,

and drove,

leaving me by the window
with my eyes at a strong stretch,

a digging of my simple irises
into another day

without the light.

He Likes When I Wear Skirts

He likes when I wear skirts,
when my calves are bare and white,
my legs freshly shaven
and moving down some crowded
street in Boston,
shiny like new sunlight
on a dark morning.

I prefer just to sleep
next to him in the daytime,
quiet and still in the daylight,
listening to the neighbors
upstairs fighting and pacing
across our bedroom ceiling.

He listens to them yell,
then finds my skirt
under the sheets,
pulls at the wrinkled
skins of 65 dying flowers,
and I just twist my bright legs
around his waist.

The Professional

She was birthed,
another bloody
          rose from between your

    legs

    and with brains
and baby hand salad,

she did not smile,
but tied an apron to your waist,

          Mommy-Mommy, give me a little peace

    but you just slid off the bed,
wiped off the guts,

and threw
    one
        round
            perfect
                apple

    at her bleating chest.

Death Mark

I have a mark which covers
the entirety of my right wrist.

It's a splotch of brown and green,
a treetop,
a lamb,
a shadow,
a wax of misery cloud.

The mark circles the most
tender portion of my body,
and I wonder if it was once a place
to drag hooks,
jagged pieces of glass,
or horny metal.

Even over 1000 years ago,
I was never the type
to be shot
with bullet or arrow.

I was probably found
hanging from a tree branch,
sipping a poison,
or drowning
in the bathwater.

All of my lives
gather into this mark
as hot words never spoken,
but understood.

I will hold my wrist
above my head,
and claim it as my heart.

The Rabbit

A brown rabbit rests his plump bottom in the mud,
separates his front paws, separates his needs,
as Rain, two inches thick, so unlike the month of June,
pleads with his fur to get into that meat,

and I watch from my window, make my own plans
to bathe outside, just a little clean,
just a little pound of waiting,
just a little stone for the turning over, and then

off he goes!

Just like that.

To Hurricane Juan, 1985

I was still fighting the algae in my mouth
when a man made of silver wagged
his tongue at my skirt.

He bent his metallic-crusted skin at me.
He folded his body down the middle
to an almost collapse and then

slobbered, "Don't you know, kid?
The sun never goes down in New Orleans."

I have seen this city lay down,
its sex bright
atop a great flood.

I have known the snakes who have slithered
'round the legs of the marching surviving.

The pelicans still fly at night.
The city will continue in its found dark,
the rain falling as slapping quarters

to embrace the crying sidewalks.

The snow jar

I am caught inside
    the snow jar,
covered in my own
    shit.
The icicles above me
form arrows, point toward
the remnants
of my first
    true regret.

White is not white anymore.

Pure is not pure.

The days look long, plastic, scratched.

I miss you over
    and over
and over,
a cycle,
a flight between NY
    and LA.

I have left you, shining and cosmic,
    I have left you in 2009,
and now everything we know
is trapped with me
    inside of this jar,
and everyone

everyone

everyone

is different.

Baumkuchen

We grew in inches then, and our
warm enemies were created
in the smashing and the busted fruit
of German tree cakes.

Our homes were made of pumpkins,
and we rolled them to
chase the front of rain,
orange and pale sweet,
held by the chubby hands of girls
above the drown line.

With barefoot splatter, we
carried food in clear sacks
out to the forest, where plants once
grew in the cracks of tea cups,
but now everything was slaughtered,
murdered, cut dead,
by the Hurricane.

The corpses of trees bent
brown backs
and held their wet bark
against our dark flats of hair.

The clover, white and spriggy,
now gone.

The wind, air,
now gone,

but we still had the taste of cake in our mouths.

Forever 19

for Christopher

You weren't alive like most people.

You were a wild bowl that somehow managed
to stay upright,

a clash of sound, early and pure
against the hard wall of morning,
a bright muscle,
stretched and bent completely backwards.

You were a friend,
a similar drop of blood,
the child I knew,
now forever 19.

These were the reasons I gave,
with a slender slashing
of my heart,
why I never
made it to your funeral,

but sat on a back porch,
1500 miles away
from the cold body I did not want to view,

with the thought that you were still there,
still sitting next to me.

She Moves As I Move

When I saw her hair move,
I was reminded of how I can move,
we can move,
because she does move like
brown pumping splitting heart.

There is a walking bridge.
I have seen it move over the city.
We were there together once.
I saw her on it,
moving inside that great cage.
She moved her head,
she moved her mouth, she moved.

She asked if the walls were built,
if that cage was built,
to prevent the movements,
to stop the movers from moving,
jumping, steaming, toppling off the bridge.

I said, *I guess so,* then I just
watched her move, felt my own move,
then felt sad
that all of our movements are only temporary,
that we must one day stop moving.

Then we moved away, we moved away.
I saw her moving as she left,
a walking, moving, brown,
carousing, galloping, steering heart
that just moved as I was moving
and left anyway.

Last Song for Minot

The last gasp of Minot slithers down red hands,
ears, throats,
atop the souls of crestfallen people.
Its saunter stalks past the wind-bruised garages,
the bloodless dirt yards, the dismantled streets.

What is it that attempts to rupture, to birth itself
from a cracked mound in the road?

Is it the burial of a lone red deer, that last hope
of the animal's unearthing, one hairy hoof to plow tar,

or simply the struggle-pop of ground where snow once
cried it's thick dry tears,
and now the earth grieves its absence?

The wind is of no use as it labors its breathing
over a child's beaten hair,
or passes its asthma through the stark tree,

Gasp. Gasp. Gasp.

Her chest is fading quickly, collapsing as the sunflower
with the first touch of frost,

the dying sounds of no revolution,
the symptoms of a bigger disease,

the misconception that depletes the worthiness
of simplicity in a humble rain,
an echoed scream into nothingness,
one determined weed,

and the sun-cloud,
the last dance in a shower of light
over that cruel, yet beautiful plain.

Invisible Night

The sun was whole,
a full circle that never died,
and never went away,
but it would crack slightly
every evening,
leak its red cherry juice
into the shy streets.

It was beautiful.

Our drinking then was excellent,
much like the standard of impeccability
that summer,

as the days were spent
with a fat cluster of flowers from the 2.99 bin,
wrapped in plastic,
the color of a ferris-wheel at midnight.

We kept our hands busy with glasses,
lifted them to the dictator of light,
and let our ghosts slobber along,
grow brighter with the days.

The wine made us stronger.

We buzzed from each room,
let the piss fill the toilets,
and stripped off our clothes
to feel alive,

to be closer in paradox,
naked in the abuse of yesterday and tomorrow,
to feel the erect touch of one more
invisible night.

Waterless

Terror was a flash that slipped through her
like warm milk.

She wanted to reach him,
shatter his dead skin into a million
little mirrors,

but she just sat there,
waterless,
in her black hat,
black dress,
next to her remaining children,
quiet.

The Husband,
still wrapped inside a crushing
black morning,
had straddled his son's bed,
and attempted to breathe life back
into an empty body.

His eyes,
still waterless,
could not focus on the box
in front of him.

(He could still feel
the glass inside his mouth.)

Machine

The strict shape of a bone is masculine.
It will sit in your hands like a tiny god
with structure and purity.

Its perfectness can be brought and held
to a white wall, white bone,
where wall meets bone's eye stare.

On a perfect bone there are no red corners to clean,
no wet drooping parts to untangle.
You rip them from your body.

Bones now fly, striking white steel wall,
splintering out perfect miniatures.

From the body obscene, white juts out
without a single blood drop.

You do not scream. You become dead matter. You are machine.

Long Bones

She said she could smell the
strength from within you,
could feel the red climb your meat
like a ladder
as you flew down the stairs,
your breath coated in beer
and the euphoria of wings.

Mother,
how thick was your marrow
as your head bent like a god,
and split apart from itself
as you crashed into the wall
at the bottom of the steps
in front of your young daughter?

Was your marrow shooting thick
through your bones,
heart as swollen as a bare orange
in the hand of a little blues singer
who thought the moon
was too bright in that moment,
slicing past the window,
a reflection of your chaotic speed?

She was right.
It was all too brilliant,
the light just perfect
for this head-dance,
and it was just an instant,
she said,
with the flapping of great wings,
you,
at the top of the stairs,
being the angel,
becoming the devil-bird,
cracking the air with your long bones.

Neighbors

She used to wave at me from her balcony,
her breasts swinging and flinging
at each other like wild boar.

She was a massive woman with the steady
arch of whale back, an ass as big as the earth,
and now she is gone.

I would listen to her stomp,
her legs bold as they blazed
through the apartment above mine.

When my electricity popped and went black,
she invited me up for a beer,
and that was when I first noticed
how birds found a home in her,
diving beneath and making sweaty her corrupt breasts.

I found out the loud clangings that rained down
on my ceiling in the middle of the night
were simply a congregation of her sins
as they dropped, great swords to her floor.

She is gone now,
replaced by others much smaller,
but I still think of her random fucks that would wake
me from sleep,
her bed creaking above mine,
my insides jumping with sticky tacky.

I used to heave my books at my ceiling,
her bedroom floor,
and watch as the sounds of her fucking
mixed with the falling of Musgrave, Plath, or Cummings.

She and they, only words pushing,
entwining, to kick me firmly, solidly,
in a lonely gut.

Off the Highway

The black-wood house
is poised to cry
over this winter. Defeat
bunches around the door
like cellulite,
fattening the corners,
rounding its posture. It
looks like a grandmother,
with the slow snow-snore
of a wounded tiger,
broken and purring.

Air Bright

The Nashville night held the weight of bone.

We walked the sidewalks with the slow
warm crawl of flowers *finally able to breathe.*

In the bar we knew nothing except glossed wood,
yellow light, and the dark taste of beer.

You flirted with the bartender and won us free shots,
your hair, a black bird already flying.

We were, together, a new birth of skeletons
air bright through ribs.

We had nothing else to learn.

Say Hello to No

All the houses were lined up the same,
all the roofs pointed in the same upwards direction,
and all the yards grew exactly the same

except for ours.

Our house stood alone,
just as a mouth that waited wide for a bug,
or a stranger that stopped to peek through a glass.

Our roof sagged.
The yard was made of dirt.
I would squish my toes in it after rain,
run in it barefoot.

The workers in summer
always wailed their hammers like guns,
but I still ran with naked feet
until one day
the trees spit at me,
the sky glared, and
all the little flowers called me names.

I had stepped on a nail.

My father,
much younger then,
softer,
stood over me,
shoulders square,
legs braced,
one hand on the end of the nail,
the other on the back of my young foot,

he
yanked
it
out.

My mouth remained clamped down,
tight as a fish and
hard as a cry,
for much longer than
it was gone from my body.

I learned that I would have to accept no,
welcome no,
if I was to live the same,
stay the same, and
be the same as all the others.

A Devil Says to Me

I stand on a pile of soot with a devil.

He tells me I am the damned,
a flat footed horse,
a piece of hollowed wood,
a great big thing without a cough.

He tells me that inside my itching bones
there is a flare that shoots up,
needles my skin into the empty shaking sky.

Empty, he tells me, empty.
I am not afraid.

This is not disaster.
It is a thing quite alright,
a rain that is all and everything,
all parts, all madness,
a wash of cool wind.

How
that devil
loves
to feel me
erupt,

using the opportunity
to dig inside my wave electric
and find blood for pearls,
peelings of nasty
that flake from my throat.

He does not care
that I can be spoken like porcelain,
using gray, clear sounds,
the rain that hits tin cans.

He does not care

for my pristine prim of entrails,
the quiet that persists.

He just says, girl,
you are a muffled sound
in a box.

What will that devil do
if my heart split into five,
each little piece,
a shriek that crashes from my fingernails,
my front tooth, a pulse
to match the extracting light,
a throb inside my open womb mouth,
alive and ugly?

That devil, he just turns to me
and says----

lie.

I Found God While Watching Frank Wash the Dishes

He stands devoutly
at the sink,
his bare feet rummaging
across the floor
for reassurance that it is whole
and still there.

He performs a baptism
on our dinner dishes
from the night before,
his hands uncontrollable,
wild birds among the suds.

His arms elongate,
dip the plate
into the dreary warm water.

I see the earth shake a little
from the kitchen window.

He drags a wash rag
across the outside
of a wine glass,
his fingers splayed,
a religious history
over our leftover damnations
and offenses.

I watch the light shift
through the open screen
and enlighten
his chest and shoulders
as he pounds
another clean fork
into the dish drainer.

His face becomes
the river of my body
under the light,
milking me straight
and refined back to faith.

Pacifist Afternoon

There was a bird deep-nested
in your winter beard.

A bird,
flapping,
alive,
is far too hostile a presence
for the precious pacings
of your clock-handed face.

I want to eat questions
off of you
for Sunday dinner.

We can wrap together
in linoleum truce,
make our small fires
from the kitchen floor.

The Quiet Room

Love remains belly-hidden,
the cocked neck of nothing,
as the stomach, long, blind, and forever,
poses as a highway for quiet thumbs,
but no thumbs have ever been willing,
and I remain untouched.

When a book goes unread it turns into a body,
a woman,
a dry poison of scattered lady parts,
a block of dead air,
an empty bladder that cannot let,
flow,
nor drain any of its usual tendencies.

Oh, to be a fresh fuck!
A name, a date, an idea,
one drop of finger, toe, or chest,
one man,

a waste of time.

The Threat

Outside the window
a red peel of blood
crusts the early morning snow
and the birds fire up like sirens.
My kitchen is bold,
waits for the gun to drop.
The crunch of his big feet approaches,
and his bang-bang
echoes across the tiles,
ready.

Choking on the Rope

The floe
of the room
slicked down
the flatiron
of your hospital
bed.

Your hair,
pancaked
and gray,
stiff
like the bottom
of a boat,
froze to the
loose blanket
of your face.

Your mouth
slipped
behind your ear
to rest,
empty,
on your pillow.

I saw
your face
flash younger,
like Marilyn Monroe
on a calendar,
on a wall
somewhere warmer,
brighter.

I wanted
to pick you up,
75 years old,
I wanted
to pick you up,

rock you
forward
and back,
sing hallelujah.

But I did not.

I tucked
into a corner
of the blood
jet wall,
I pushed
my feet
harder
into the pulsing
life
of carpet,
but the force
of objects
failed me.

I
died
a little
with
you.

When I
opened
my mouth,
I felt
Nothing
trample out,
and Nothing
bound
quick and
blind
to your
dangling feet,

like a little girl
stained
with sulfur
and choking
on
the
rope.

That Breakfast in Savannah

He told us his mother threw
a pot of boiling water
on his face
when he was just 7 years old,

so now he chooses
to sleep under swirls
of Spanish moss,
on top of freshly cut grass,
next to a park bench.

He ignores the corpse-less
hearses that rev their engines
on the other side of the fence.
He lets them take their positions
in the streets,
says that all beggars play fathers
to homeless burn victims
who ride bikes.

We discussed his freedom
that morning,
on a tall southern porch.
Our full plates filled our eyes,
white as moon circles,
perfect with gravy,
the reds of our gently sliced tomatoes
bleeding heavy into the morning.

Then we walked
like sweating flowers
through Bonaventure,
tiptoed around the famous graves
of artists and children,
but hoped with the sweet honey
of a last hope,
to catch one more glimpse
of the boy with the scarred face,

cruising on old wheels
through an ancient afternoon sun,
wrecking us
with his little grass song.

That Dinner in Savannah

The evening was a damp sponge.
Strange birds plucked at it,
passed it back and forth between their beaks.
We watched from our outdoor table,
fascinated by so many sky-eating creatures.

Across from me, she happily traced circles
of night back toward her eyes,
fingered the dip of her spoon,
waited for the meal to arrive.

College kids swirled their umbrellas,
oblivious to the wonders and miracles
that spilled from the shoulders of Savannah's sunset.

God, it feels good to be free tonight.

When my beer finally arrived,
I sucked it down quickly,
stood as a scarecrow for the birds.
She joined me. The birds ignored us.
It was good. It was clean.

We did not care what the others thought.

Where Does the Light Go?

I cannot remember exactly how long it has been
since I last watched the sun go down
simply for the beauty of seeing.

Five years, maybe more,
since I watched its descent
every evening in the summer
from the porch of 1000 ghosts,
as I spoke of curfews and
attempted to tan my skinny knees.

I understood that specific falling of light.
It understood me.

I am reminded of this as
pink washes the house of the neighbor.

They sit outside, drink wine, smoke cigarettes,
and let the blind dog bark.

The dog cannot see the pink.
He is happy anyway.

I take a drive through the neighborhood
and watch all the lonely people outside.
They look toward the source of settling day,
the orange and gray sky.

It looks like rain.

I drive past a man who stands in his small garden.
He does not look up.
He is perfectly happy to consider the bush in front of him.

I do not consider this an act of blindness.

Never Swallowed the Kamikaze

In the photograph, she is only thirteen.
She has braces, but her smile remains
unhindered by their cage.
Her lips curl up around the metal
like a wind-bruised umbrella.
She drapes her dark brown hair
royal and long like a cape,
lets it shield her small bra-less breasts
from peeking through her thin shirt.
Her bones are tight and intact.
She still believes in the red strength of her blood
and that snow will fall every December.
She does not fear that the sweetness
between layers of cake will fade,
or that the sun will lose its warm cocoon.
Her eyes flicker, but she does not know yet
how to cry.
She has never fallen between the dead faces
of glasses, bottles, or pipes.
She has never swallowed the kamikaze,
or felt its blast rip her bladder
from her defenseless body.
No, my mother just glistens on paper,
holds up two fingers in a peace sign.

Highway 83 North, 3 a.m.

The night is black pudding, is a funnel,
is the bottom shelf of my common sense.
I have never felt more small.

The graceful windmills of day have turned into
giant monstrosities of red light horror.
200 feet tall, they surround me, a gaggle of angry mothers.
They watch me, undress me from their fields.

I cannot see the deer, but I know they are there.
They hop on their deer hooves and think
deer things. Their muscles, their grace, terrify me.

When I was a girl, my father put deer in the stew
and told me it was beef. I think of this as the big rig
trucker flashes me with his brights.
I am vulnerable to his will.

I keep my eyes straight ahead, dissect the road
in terms of miles and speed. When the city lights
of home spread open like a blanket on the dark prairie,

I become powerful again. I become as red as the
blinking lights of wind, as black as the terrible sky.

The Lost Story of Mary

I have a living grandmother,
but I call her Mary Holds onto Death.
She lives as a hairy old witch,
alone, hiding inside the forest of her crumbling house.

She screams "Puh!"
at the cracks in the roof-tipping oaks.
She screams "Puh!"
at the dead Husband in her creaky chair.

Her windows are packed in leafy bibles,
the pages, gone.
She rides a fat pig from her bedroom
to her bathroom,
bangs on the floor with her cane.

She cries, "God bless the child,"
and jerks on the nuzzle.
The pig squeals in delight.

But Mary will not hobble past
the opening to her kitchen,
because inside there is a bright gold couch
that stretches long, a fallen log,
across the floor.

It is made of hard plastic,
and she remembers the terrible squeak
it would make
as all her daughters slid
in and out of it each night, long ago.

All the scents of past
are still licking the material,
the smell of quick careless unforgiving girls,
their berried breath, underarm sweat,
salty hair, and baby oiled skin.

Mary holds onto death,
shields her breasts from God,
and now from the women who do not remember.

greater than

He was an animal of celestial ability,
with skin that itched for another turn
of the tire,
another song of his pants,
a day,
a vowel-like motion,

but his roads were drugged and loose,
and maybe he was on something greater than toxic
as he gripped that far country by its horns and spoke
with train tracks that lined his throat,

the smoke never dies
in the French that left him.

Maybe he can find his love again,
that sprung out sparrow of foreign ancestry,
and catch it, bleeding down into his hands,

a buttered particle of wisdom.

Heights

I like to stand on tall bridges
because I am not afraid of heights.

With a mile of cold beneath me,
a mile of thought around me,
I never think to jump,
to cradle that black of thought
in my arms like a child,
and hold my foot out over the stale air.

No, I keep thought only waist high,
mid-level, around the spot
where father packs his gun,
the blot of hip where I can control
and soothe it.

I keep thought small and trivial,
circles and straight lines,
and only the easiest of dictionary entries.

I think of the many feet that have walked
the pass, the many rains that have washed
the droppings of birds,
and the many sun rises, sunsets,
that have shone and declined against
the steel hand rails.

I think of the little farm I visited as a child,
where I slept in a barn in the company of a horse
and three brown cats,
where I kept thought tight
and smooth in the rafters,
because I am not afraid of heights.

The Bottle Tree

for Jessica

A girl wants the bottle tree, she wants
it raining
down on her like spring, she
wants to see the tide, I can see
her small head under her curl of long hair, she
holds her hair like a misery
her head is a hot
one, the tree looms
it is big
it snorts
it is small
it leaks she
can smell the daddy on it, she
wants the tree near her
skin
the hotness of sun on bark
the pile of flowers by her bare feet, her
head piles thoughts like a misery
it rains
down on her
like spring
there is a sun on the hot pile
the big daddy tree and her hair her hair her
hair was so curly, it curved her bottom
it was long and hot
it smelled like looked like felt
like daddy
like spring
she moved the hair to her arms, a hot one
on her arms
the snorting
was like daddy
the tree was big
it was small
the sun hit like spring
raining down.

Circles

The motel carpet crooked like an elbow
underneath my neck, a mattress leaned
like an abandoned dress against the window.

We waited out the storm.

The wind howled like a cat in heat.
It was a bloody sound, a filthy sort of racket.

During the eye, I walked with my father
out onto the balcony. Broken glass grew
like mushrooms in the mud.
Treetops slept on the roofs of cars.

My father bounced on his feet,
said something truly introspective like,
"holy shit!"

My mother stayed inside. The eye
did not thrill nor impress her.

It was quiet out there,
with only the cautious sound of opening doors
and the tender steps of the curious,
peeking their heads out of their numbered rooms
like animals coming out of caves.

I placed my faith and my small fingers
inside the tight circles of the buttons
that lined my shirt,
knowing they weren't going anywhere,

they were safe.

The Last Whale Song in the Badlands

Too many oceans have sunk here,
left their old love notes,
morning yawns,
and rub of whale-belly scar
against the hidden hearts of the hills.

Their tops mark the valley
and roast like giant raisins,
wrinkled pulse-muscle skins
that dent and swell
with our feet.

The cries of animals,
yesterday's whale song
and today's buffalo scream,
still echo and suspend
in monuments of combed air.

We are rushed into the sound
like birds of wave,
feeling the grassed music,
entering the strong blood
of the voices' tornado crash.

The animals still call for her,
that shy naked neck of heaven,
to reveal her smooth tips
and milky undersides,
to dip enchanted
and release her calm tears
onto the sun bruised mud.

Pillars of all the old rock ladies hold us,
the animals build up their chorus,
and we become the noise,
we are the wind,
we sing with the mouths of whales
the last song in the Badlands.

the hand job

as I held his penis
in my spit slicked hand
I thought about how I forgot
to buy more lotion
at the store today
which made me remember
I ought to buy new
windshield wipers
because it's so hard to drive
in a blizzard
with broken ones
like last month
when I had to pull over
on the highway
like a scared deer
to peel the ice off
of those black rubber blades
and how that police car
slowed down
but did not stop
as it passed me
shooting a sharp rain of snow
in my freshly washed hair
and maybe I should get
a new shampoo
because the one
I have been using lately
just hasn't been getting
the job done.

I died with it all so easily

One night,
I died with it all so easily.

I completed the big cave-in,
let the dry
dry
and the heat
heat.

I massaged simplicity
into my earth bones.

Complexity
stayed close,
shuddered and spewed
near my cold ribs.

The random power
of circumstance,
I swallowed down,
one handful of loose change.

My stains resisted
resistance,
drained my eyebrows
into pitch,
created a mean mess
of my face.

I let time
time out,
I let rhyme
rhyme,
and colors
color.

I felt music flutter,

the midnight birds finally chirped
and that damn cricket
outside my window finally
realized that summer was over.

I let him in,
right into my home,

and he died proudly,
with no disaster
in his little croak,

claimed death
as his only reward.

Don't Go, Janie

Icicles clump
to what is left
of her hair,
and her veins,
once swollen
and ripe, red
Christmas lights,
now shrink
and tangle
in death's black
chords.

Loud moans
swoop from her
mouth
like owls
to branches,
and I place
my hands on hers.

A Red Horse

Spring is a red horse that stands alone in the grass,
unable to graze.

I could drape a dying arm across his back,
settle in like a thick molasses,
nudge his nose to the ground,
and guide his hunger,
but I am not a warm circle of want.

I was created cold,
made from snow and wax.

Spring brings me heat,
grows tall sunflowers up my legs,
but I cannot be burned from these small fires,
or the sparks that fly from his hooves.

I tug at the reins.
I will only clobber his horse beating heart.

Papers

Love was the color of rooster blood
letting slow over a set of special ankles,
the sound of one clap tough in the dark,
or a 2 minute thunderstorm on the thin roof,
just enough, just enough.

I was careful.

I did not eat the rooster in the daytime.

I was quiet on the staircase,
a shred of fitful sleep,
a steady moving disaster of hate notes.

The house I wanted,
now just a brain on a couch, an inconvenience.

All the little piggies could not see.

Piggies on the midnight cue,
piggies on the dumb,
piggies stuck in syrup movements
too blind to see, see, see,
me coming.

I burned the papers brighter, brighter
than his voice on Mondays,
deeper, deeper than his sting,
harder, harder than his heart.

I was careful.

I burned away his everything.

Butter soft bones, he was a long line of boys,
pigeon shit.

I did not eat the rooster in the night-time.

I was careful.
I turned a little head.

Modern Owls

after Renoir's Dance at Bougival

That cruel spin of skirt layers
was not subtle, it blamed
and wounded the eyes of modern owls,
slaughtered them from
their own sky-homes.

That belligerent dress
extracted a madness,
a nocturnal necessity,
draped the saucered vision
in fierce reminders

of never had, never be,
never had, never be,
never had, never be,
never will have.

Peering at this sour time
of strangers dancing too close,
it became apparent in the cloth
versus the straw,
the sad flop of her mouth,
the delicate intruder,

that the life of another spin
will not rectify,
will not save,
will not preserve,
will not blind the birds
from seeing, seeing, seeing her histories,
her devastations,
her heart
beating out of her withdrawn eyes,
the night sky at her back,
cold and piercing.

the church door

the church door stood locked,
white and tall, steadfast
in Hornitos, California.
little girls came
to kneel before it
and place rocks on the steps.
they did not recognize
their various punishments--
they only knew of the beauty
and purity of the strong wood.
the door remained closed,
and the lock remained tight,
but they still came
with wounds on their knees.

Mersin

The water was mischievous that night
beside Mersin.

It was a wicked grin from the shore,
or a rumpled sheet stretched over
an ocean of midnight bed.

The moon watched patiently over
the dancers' excited bodies
like a distant shark.

Fires burnt the ends of the ladies'
scarves as they swung
past the flames.

The fabric exploded from their heads
in reds and oranges,
greens and blues, stitched-on tulips
and pomegranates.

The shiny women all reflected
in the heat,
their bare feet smacked
the wooden beams of the platform.

The men loved them
and touched each of them
with warm hands.

An American woman watched
the colors ignite
from the 20th floor above, alone.

She was too afraid to leave
her young daughter unattended
in the small condo room,
around the delicate straw beds,
and the sensitive windows

that swung open
to bright evening air
with one tap of small finger.

Her other daughter was somewhere
down inside that heavy swaying mass,
being fed little bits of strange fruit
from a boy with a sinful smile.

The dancing ladies swept by
the unchaperoned children,
their thin skirts floating a hot breeze
against two sets of bare legs.

The girl had plunged one hand deep
into the clean pilaf
and tasted it.

The boy swiped a bottle of liquor
and took off like a jet
across the vibrating sand.

The surf opened its watery mouth
in an approving yawn of laughter,
and the daughter wiggled a little
to the thunder of music.

Happy Joe

I was a mixture of cracked yellow brick,
severed limbs,
paint and crashed fences, femur and scapula,

raw meat.
We would take to the floor
of abandoned apartment buildings,
touch hair, and play
with bottles of glue and motor oil,
beer cans and salt water.

I was 19.

I knew everything about vodka and the shoulders of boys.

You liked that.

The first time you came on my tits
your eyes parted like blue birds
leaving the ground.

Tell me what you want.
Your balls pressed my thigh.

I wanted more.

The snow fell in the trees like hammers,
waiting to ice us down.

Now you are married.
Now you go hunting and play with your dogs.

I bet your hands are still the same.

I bet you taste exactly the same.

The Determined Undermining of Summer

I lust for a good summer rain--unexpected,
brutal,
a killing.

I want it mean and pissed,

its wail
challenging the parting with sky.

He crawls onto my back--
Can you fuck a feeling? I ask,

bare now, undiscovered.

I leave with a cry and a new kind of story.

My father always told me
things are never
quite as clean
as they might first appear.

It always burns a little when it goes in

When I was young
I had a Christmas ornament
made from glazed dough.

It was molded into the shape
of a little girl in a red dress
by the hands of a woman
whose grandmother was once a slave.

Every year it would melt a little
on the tree's lights,
and this was the perfect time
for me to take it down,
to smell the salt
and the hands that kneaded it.

Sometimes my pink tongue
would curiously
touch the girl's misshapen feet,
or the black of her hair,

and I would fight the endless urge
to take a bite.

I would then think of that woman
in the streets of Charleston,
her hips wide and free,
as she wrapped the tiny ornament
carefully in tissue,
handed it to me,

and smiled through bright crooked teeth.

Up the Whiskey Tree

You climb down from your whiskey tree
long enough to ask,

What do you know about fucking?

Not much these days,
I respond,
my hands tightly clasped in my lap.

I try to change the subject to beer,
the Red Sox,
or the dangers of using too many metaphors.

I avoid the topics
of unfamiliar organs,
hairy legs,
dildos,
doggie style,
reverse cowgirl,
Monkey Pulls the Turnip.

You dry hump the grass next to my feet,
say, *I feel lucky this afternoon.*

I grow excited in spite of myself,
imagine your mouth firmly positioned
around my nipple.

My panties grow damp,
but you just turn around,
climb back up your whiskey tree,

and leave me panting in the grass.

A Telescope and Other Instruments of Persuasion

The tall prairie grasses scratched
at their naked butt-cheeks. They

did not notice the touch.

They just kept walking through it, walking
toward the infinite sky, walking
to nowhere that I knew about.

This notion made me squirm in my seat,
at 90 miles an hour, I squirmed
in my seat, and I felt like dancing

to the song of their people,
the vibrations slapping the road,
brown.

It was the morning after
my first look in a telescope,
and now everything was a little far away,
a little lost,
a little blurry.

I remembered how big the sky was,
how I could see one perfect star

closer, it's fiery gases moving,
but I was greedy. I wanted a satellite.

I longed to see one hover over the frame,
unnatural

and prying.

Was I the instrument now?

The song of their people continued,
the vibrations alive on the road,
brown.

I kept driving.

to business men everywhere

The bathroom has one brick wall.

Once painted white, it now looks yellow,

and in the cracks: baby heads, stretched clouds, half paw prints, deformed potatoes.

I see what I want to see.

Don't ask me to scrub it.

The Flying Birds

I asked him, *Why is it*
that we write
when nobody really wants
us to?

but the answer was estranged

placed
gently
on the backbone
of a long silence

while the night purred
around us

and the sky
filled
with a crowd

of high flying birds

that we could not see
but knew were there.

Skin

It was a disservice to the skin,
fingering those poems in the hot room.

When I emerged, red and crazy,
blisters swelled up over the length of my body

like angry spitting babies.

I brought the lotions, creams,
natural tonics made of honey,
asparagus, and pomegranate,
I brought them all to the table
and screamed for clarity of flesh.

Stop it now, he muttered,

and now,
it is only a mark of heat, he claims,

but I know better.

I go to brush the wild knots from my hair,
I tear at them with shaking hands
in front of the mirror.

I swivel my dying dandelion head.
Pivot. Pivot.
From every angle a stranger.

It says a lot
about a person
once they admit
the terrible face
that reflects back at them
(open mouthed
and wasteful)
will never be their own.

I swirl through these plain rooms
unlike any meat hurricane
you have ever seen.

I flap my arms insanely,
stick pages from books
and childhood photographs to walls

to remind me of smooth skin
and all the women I used to be.

Now I hide my cranberried flesh.
Now I rumble like muffled thunder.

The Bird

The bird,
small and brown,
made a home above my door

but I do not know why.

I open the door and I slam it shut,
my daily comings and goings,

and that little thing,
he gets pissed and flies from his nest

every single time,

but he keeps coming back
to his home,

sun or flood,

he always has the faith
to come right back.

Scavenger

At 2 a.m. a cat streaks across the road,
a wiggling animal in its mouth.

My car slices through the June night taking with it
the final light of unaccounted stars.

Like the last blueberry greedily swiped from the bowl,
the evening squanders clarity, remains perfectly round.

I am left with only a back pocket of burnt paper
that only a fool would call meaningful.

What would the single sleeping bird do?

Letters

I used to write letters to boys
when I was in the 8th grade,

boys with mischievous smiles
but kind eyes.

I would ask them if they knew of the 3 small moles
that formed a handle on my shoulder,

"like the one on the Big Dipper," I would write,
"not the Little,"

and I would describe the fear I felt as I stood
in doorways and sat at school desks
and wondered if that handle would catch
on the wood,

only to leave me hanging,
my knees chubby and exposed,
my hands dangling uselessly
at my sides.

I only ever got one response:

"April,

don't look up."

It Will Only Hold For So Long

I hide my giant-ism behind a group of soul-trees,

and grossly trimmed, perfectly shaped,
they provide an easy shade,

but the fur of their bark skins my fingers,
and their steepness holds no candle
to the grave I'm digging for myself,

the depths of which cannot be measured
by any mathematics.

Bats, black terrible things,
singe through my protections,
fly at my eyes,
the clicking creatures of night,

to form a bleeding autumn
every day in the tiger of my mind,

but I still hide, and I hide well,

long after the trains have plowed
through the churches,
long after the wheat of my brain
has been thoroughly gleaned.

I remain the insignificant giant,
squeaking truth and justifying fear,

to force the shelter of the trees
to remain stitched on my chest,
to dance the leaves mightily,
a thin distraction from the terror

I so often keep.

Marriage

We married in broad daylight

in front of the looking-trees
and under the watchful sun
and right next to the baby purple flowers
that seemed to open their heads

and in the eye-line of everyone else
all dressed in black
with big dramatic hats

we married

and then we drank too much
at the reception,

wherein I locked myself in the bathroom
like a prisoner in black and white stripes
like an infant butterfly without a cocoon

and when you coaxed me out

we fucked on the white bed
my lace knitted lingerie wrinkled
and in disrepair

while you held my knees above my head
and said you were so glad I was your wife

then you dug your nails in deep
into the meat of my thighs

and I cried from what I said
was only a flesh wound

but really
it was much more than that.

Old Charleston--a Memory

The strange taste of Old Charleston
is almost to the rot,
too sweet to tongue,
too distant to believe,
now ready to be packed up,
fried in coffin-skin,
boiled around a southern flag.

But the aged air falls into mouth once in awhile,

and history cleans mouth out once in awhile,

like that faint mint of winter,
when sister was born
into the rain slapped sky,
and the water sloshed free and cool
over arms and bare legs,
the water was friendly,
dotted the wood porch,
dotted the sidewalk.

Remember the city was alive,
the ooze of blood imagined in sweaty streets,
people damp, smiling,
beauty, history, captured
by cameras, paint,
minds.

Remember the brown woman's flesh was dough,

was straw and sugar working the muscle.

Remember the taste of summer,
green and white,
as children picked clover
from the shade of trees.

In the Neighborhood

No one saw the dog
until it jerked its helpless body
in the middle of the road.

It fought for life
as cars splashed by,
as a boy and a mother cried
from the sidewalk,
their tears slamming
long trains to the ground.

A man came with sadness in his eyes,
in his work boots,
in his plaid shirt and busted jeans.

He held the furry body
up against his strong one,
carried it to a dry spot of brown grass,
and rubbed the soft nose with one finger.

Spring continued to spread its water.

No Gentle Thing

It indicates from the sky,
prods at the deaf carnation of my mouth.

It bleeds into the shape
of one dead-dog cloud with white puffy tongue,

a limp but bold obstacle,
a flying tumor on the air.

Never Cross

I circled through my quiet childhood
on a white bicycle with black streamers
that flapped the stale scent
of dust and tar, smoke and burnt grass,
another day of Charleston in the spring-time.

I made circles, and circles, and circles
on the dull pavement of the same old driveway,

circles, and circles, and circles
across the street from those magical mailboxes
that glinted numbers up to 50,
a small box for each townhouse on the street,

and I longed to ride straight,
right across that dark street,
feel the wind sweep the salt from my skin,
taste the wildness of strawberries
mixed with drops of sweat
inside my mouth,

but my mother would yell through the screen door,
never cross! never cross,

as the cars and delivery trucks
main-lined the streets,
and my horse-tail of brown hair
stayed stuck to the path between my shoulders.

One day my desires grew,
changed the little girl in me,
and I claimed the rebel tastes I craved,
beat the traffic,
and raced to the other side of the road.

How tall I must have looked over there,
how long and firm,
as my feet touched the ground

on the wrong side of the street,
and those mailboxes next to me
just shined like the whole big sun,

my pedals spun on the air.

Impressions

It started before daylight, before the sun ran egg-y
over the Middle Eastern desert.

It was a Spring morning of lasts,
of last days of innocence, last chances,
and last sources of light down midnight hallways.

I knew this somehow, knew it like the cracked pieces
of sun in my hand, as all the Turkish girls
swept us into the pits of sweat that pooled under their arms,
sticky, sweet, and foreign.

I knew it when they flounced the black skirts
of their uniforms, round and whole as oranges,
and bounced their bare legs next to our cotton covered ones
in that early heat of pink light.

Later, they took us to a secret place down
a cement corridor, a place where the window
stood tall, gleaming with metal bars,
and the sun banged through the glass like a jack-hammer.

They giggled and let their Turkish words slide
from their greased tongues as they pointed
down to a group of young men on a field.

They were chasing a ball, running in shorts,
their brown legs covered in spiders of dark hair,
while they jostled between patches of browned grass.

The girl with the roundest mouth placed her fingers
on a square of that glass and looked back at me,
her eyes cool and black next to all of that sun,
and she said brokenly, "You know it! Okay?"
Then she gave me a thumbs up, her long fingers
moist and meshed together.

I wanted to tell her one million things,
ask her one million questions about life and knowing,
how that sun managed to stay so high
when there were pieces of it pulverized in my pocket,

but I just smiled back, said, "Okay."

Worth in Silver

I used to steal my mother's
ring, Class of '78 around my thumb,
bright sterling silver
of round,
with a big chunk of deep blue
shining gem in the middle.

I wore it to a Turkish school
where the gray walls devoured
any chance of sun, and the black
uniforms kept all in line
with the giant squares of metal
and cement.

The teacher at the front of the room,
tall as nails, with sharper short hair,
rapped her ruler
and screeched
to silence the class as she ran toward me,
a hungry spark in her eye,
as she grasped my hand
and cried out with a shower of Turkish
syllables.

She motioned at me
a desire to wear the ring,
and I, terrified, handed it over
without any hesitation,
and watched
as she slid the circle
of light around her dark
ring finger.

She smiled,

and popped a student over the head
with that angry ruler,
and continued her lesson in

Mathematics,
wailing that ruler
and admiring the new look
of her once bare hand,

while I sat in the chalk streaked desk
and remembered my mother
advising me about the weight of worth
between silver versus gold,

Never choose silver like I did,
you will regret it.

This is My Favorite Sky

A smattering of rain, the 8 p.m. sky
settles its back-skin like a fogged window
across the city.

The streets hum in the steam,
the summer splashes,
paints itself in a blue watercolor.

The city melts a little, slicks across the sidewalks,
slips a little deeper into the earth.

A girl, with her horse-brown hair,
a wild thing,
breathes the art of the air,
lets the gentle smoke
enter her body
and create little magics within it.

"This is no pale Virginia,"
she says,
as she crosses her legs,
a woman who knows better.

The sun soon morphs to moon,
and she sees the city plump up again,
the streets fatten, and the sidewalks dry,
expand.

She thinks the whole world
just jelled back together.

International Gothic

In afternoons,
I pretend my hair strings up
like an orchestra behind my neck,
fluting music,
as if the wind held it sky-ward
in sunlit prayer,
and then, suddenly, my body
is painted in red sashes,
bright white cloth, and the glow
of International Gothic.

I pose, majestic, on the hill,
the sun, a diamond,
the snow parting, a blood river
before my feet,
and the birds landing on my slim shoulders
to pin sparkled-jewels
to my pert breasts (with vaguely exposed
perfect nipples.)

Shortly afterward,
the ice patch proves
a little too slippery
for my clumsy feet,
and I topple onto my quite normal ass,
(with my just average breasts)
to become the same rather unimportant lady,

late for work again.

4th of July

The day had shed bits of skin
and the pieces were drying in the yard,
warmed by the sound of explosions,
the big boom-basts
that vibrated our shoddy hilltop.

We were hung through there,
skewered on a stranger's front steps,
eying the darkness
and listening to the thunder circle the cliff,
but there was nothing to look at
except the stars
that spotted the charbroiled sky.

People with blankets writhed on the ground,
expectant for a slice of beauty
to unwrap and expose itself to all of us,
simply because beauty is so hard to keep new,
ripe, and gentle
in these parts of the country.

I saw those wishing bodies
white and open in front of me, aimed at the night,
perfect still, even in their longing,
just like the tilt your hat gave to the grass.

I saw an entire era of summer blues
stuffed inside of one note,
one little pocket hand grenade
that could be taken out and sipped with a straw.

The fireworks never reached high enough
to be seen by any of us that evening,
but the sky slanted like a bare chest,
reached an angle of pure nudity,
and labeled itself beautiful.

What Horace Remembers

He remembers Korea
as an army of heartbeats in the dirt,
a steady tick on the earth
like a frightened chest of dog.

The war-feet of dead men
marched through the blood of ground,
with a pound-pound-pound of sprung dirt.

There were no animals awake in the mud,
he told me, but the land had a pulse.

He walked it like a dying horse
with a hand-written prayer in his pocket,
a paper magic that passed between
the dirtied hands of soldiers.

His legs, his arms, his teeth
now suffer the memory of Korea
as his knife scrapes a dish,
as he carefully folds his shirts,
blankets, and newspapers,
as he searches for a coffee filter in his quiet kitchen.

He remembers Korea
but he remembers her clearer,
his flower lady who waited on shore for him
like a peony,
full and bright in the dark.

Lid on Tight

I have never seen frangipani, ghost orchids,
or the milk that slides from the root.

I have wasted too much time sniffing in gardens,
pissing in jars.

I want to hear the sun tip-toe down my stairs,
a soft bladder in its teeth.

It will creep. It will slow its big shining feet. It will bite.

The rain will dribble on the stairs until morning.

It Broke Anyway

When she went

I was the
absurdity of a glass
slipping from my hands
to a sink,

and it broke anyway.

She knew
and she knew
what she did not want,

to become
the body stewing,
molding,

in the eyes of the vibrant.

Let me tell you something,
that woman
had no use for canes
or any other walking device,

she kept
her own legs useful
until that cancer
began to roughly overtake
and eat, eat, eat.

What
and
how goes
that nightly oxygen tank?

The tool,
a breathing mechanism
that gave her the life

for one more

fuck off
and fuck you
to the world.

Does that mass of wires and tubes,
that big machine,
shift in a corner cobwebby somewhere?

How old, old, old!

My grandmother
had no time for old,
no matter how her face crinkled
or her days folded like an apron around
her middle.

For a touch of that certain type of wrinkled,
I will never forget,
nor tire.

And to think
I had once called for
a formal undressing of my grandmother's stays.

How unnecessary,

because stay,
she will
in the kneaded rounds of his face,
in the wagging fingers of their children,

and in the trust I have welcomed into my own organs.

That was one hell of a swaddle deathbed,
and she should have
never
been denied that whiskey.

If I could
take it back,
I would have held it
on her tongue for a second longer
than her death had taken her.

For the Girl I Have Named Tonic

In New York City, the summer of 2000,

our eyes passed over one another,
briefly atop
the newspaper of a stranger.

We looked back again,
one toward the other,
as the sun rippled through us
with a rare tenderness,

and we smiled, alone.

I can still see you,
Rose-fisted on that city bench,
a wine-crawl Sunday with
French nose and hands.

You were a traveler.
You rubbed balm on your stomach.

You still purr and stretch
before me,
the shade of 1000 water color paintings.

You knew me well.

I have dreamed of the owl
you kept in your belly,
and I have heard it howl
next to me in the night,

whoo-whoo! in the sheets.

One moment of sipping
identical ice waters
from across a busy street,

60 seconds of wordless
appreciation and a crossing
of the legs,

and I knew
she knows me well.

Nipping at Heels

The mud was six inches deep,
sorrowful,

shy,

and yet,
it still drank from our ankles.

The fox,
the bobcat,
the wild watched

as we invaded the valley with our foreign shoes,

and I said to him,
It's the violins behind the thing.
It is always the instruments
behind

the thing,

and we kept walking until the owl we could
never see

grew fresh and important,

and he laid me down inside that mud

like a fork
meant to be beside the plate,

and he told me,

*You always think of the best lines
when no one is around to hear them.*

Warmth

I once died
on top of

3 other lifeless bodies

and sprawled and naked and pale green
in the shaky light

I cried out to death
to stick her head into my mouth

and when she came

I sprouted new hands and feet
above the cold ones

and climbed from the rubble of flesh
and meat

to stain the air.

I Thought of Stars

Ex-husband, your face was a well-known weapon,
as delicate as the autumn leaf cracking on the water,
as pointless as the unhatch-able egg
between the mother's legs.

I was of whipped cream flesh.
I dozed on soft white.

After midnight, as you slept hearty, I would wake
to summon Sweeter. He was your friend, your well
known friend.

As you slept, his hair dragged across my stomach,
my face,
my feet.

I used to finger his elbows.
I used to enjoy him.
I rained him.
He rained me.

Ex-husband, each morning as the sun
crept up the house-side like a spider,
each morning as you slumbered in perfect drunk slumber
20 feet away,

he came to me in your bed,

a big pale ice,
warmer than your fat clumsy hands, warmer than
that sun creeping the window.

Ex-husband, he drank from me as a dying horse,
a thirsting man finally given the tit,
and as he pulled on it with his clean teeth,
I thought of moon-shine.

I thought of stars.

Professor Zitelli's Tiny Chai Glass

In a room, between the hard ceiling
and shiny floor,
three sheep pushed their noses down.

Turkish, I thought, *maybe I am Turkish.*

Brown hands, brown feet in sandals, and men in black wool
claimed me.

She was there
with scarves painted across her body.
You have a lovely head, she said, *do not lose it.*

She held German candles, extinguished them
with the tips of two fingers.

Her face snapped—gone,
then reappeared
wide and tan,
as she folded her legs to fit inside
a tiny chai glass.

Do not scream, she said,
there is much here you do not know.

The men balanced cubes of sugar
on her forehead,
and she watched me,

a girl, upside down
and swung from that ceiling.

Thick

My stomach will not always
settle here
as this quiet pudding,

white and fatty,
sweet.
I will waste myself,

the sounds of my sugared skin,
tink-tinking,

as I scoop from bone,
flick from spoon.

Round hunks of me
will dry in the air,
fall crisp, molasses to dead grass.

I will flake my body,
make me
dim and small on the wind.

No more sad throat,
No more little bells eclipsed in snow.

My layers
once crunchy,
nectarous,

will lose their flavor
as I grow perpendicular,

your shrinking pocketful
of straight
and lean.

I will become bitter rind,
hardened,
set nude in the sun.

This is the Earth

This is the earth: wet-slick
buildings, towering slopes,
arcs, angles, crosses, cardboard boxes.

This is the earth: ugly glory,
beautiful sadness, shallow amazing,
heavy tsunami, blazing snow,
fantastic quake, bleeding mud,
traveling rain over rooftops,
windows, windshields, foreheads.

pillarsandchapels
villagescitiespeoplepeoplepeople
with faces, names, fears, wants,
lies, and bets.

This is the earth: a frame,
round and whole, the blue ball,
wicked and good, spherical sharp,
danger safesafesafe.

Hands, feet, beards,
hair, thighs, bellies, and sexual organs,
runningskiingswimmingbreathing
peeling skin blue eyes brown eyes
greengreengreen.

This is the earth: fucking, eating, death.

Stop

In mornings, the scale purrs at me
with the face of a whiskered rose.

It sees that I am naked.
It tries hard. It labors.

It opens up wide with thunder explosions
and the roar of a heavy dark bruise.

This does not stop me.
I remain devout. I am faithful.

I continue to slip old items down the long faucet
of my esophagus.

I mean it.

I want the last of the spare smoking meat.
I eat it dried and hard,

on a plain, in the hot sun,
after it has been stretched and smoked

and hung on a fence.
It is salty and warm,

just as my armpits, just as my thighs.

Can You Smell That Too?

Their suffering was seen
in eyes that glinted bright
as silver pieces found
on the boardwalk,
dimes placed
in dirty pockets of children.

It is not with the boat
where I leave my blame.

That hovel was only
the skin of the slick issue,
the brunt of the thick answers.

I fell down
at stout lines and danger hooks,
stern rods and dangling bait.

The waves,
salt,
birds,
and smell
of the ocean,
I have deemed
unimportant,
their temperatures and depths forgotten.

The only truths I hold
lived inside the shimmer
of those scales,
the way the sun hit
them with a twist of tornado light,
how the color slipped and split between
the perfect separations.

When the fish
began to bleed,

red pools pulsed
from their small agape mouths.

Their eye sockets popped,
white buttons,
disbelieving
the swarm of wretched thoughts
that hovered about the people,

the notion sensed,
death by fire.

The moon isn't the only lonesome thing

The sidewalk outside my house is lonely.
No one bothers to sweep it anymore.
We wait for the wind to scatter
the dirt and garbage
that falls absentmindedly to cracked concrete.

I think of all the other things
that spend their days alone--
all the lined up empty chairs
in a morning theater,
the uneaten food that sits on a porch
in Minnesota,
the neatly folded socks in a drawer
of my ex-husband,
unheard songs, unseen paintings,
steps never allowed to be taken,
and untouched drinks that thirst
only for themselves.

Acknowledgements

Some of these poems have appeared in *Santa Fe Review, Oak Bend Review, Full of Crow, Istanbul Literary Review, Southeast Review, Hobo Camp Review, The Rusty Truck, The Scrambler, Triggerfish Critical Review, The Legendary, Pot Luck Magazine, Danse Macabre, erbacce, Gutter Eloquence, Red Fez, Boston Literary Magazine, The Orange Room Review, Leaf Garden Press, deuce coupe, Guerilla Pamphlets, Durable Goods, Every Reason Zine,* and *Out of Our.*

About the Author

April Michelle Bratten was born in Marrero, Louisiana. She received her Bachelor's degree in English Literature from Minot State University in Minot, North Dakota. April was a finalist for the Best of the Net award in 2009 and was nominated again in 2010. She was also nominated for the 2010 Pushcart Prize. Her work has been widely published in both print and online, including the journals *Istanbul Literary Review, Santa Fe Literary Review, San Pedro River Review, Southeast Review, Gutter Eloquence, Kill Poet, The Orange Room Review,* and *Dark Sky Magazine* among others. She co-edits and writes book reviews for the online literary journal *Up the Staircase Quarterly,* which can be found at upthestaircase.org.

NeoPoiesis: *a new way of making*

1) in ancient Greece, poiesis referred to the process of making: creation - production - organization - formation - causation

2) a process that can be physical and spiritual, biological and intellectual, artistic and technological, material and teleological, efficient and formal

3) a means of modifying the environment and a method of organizing the self, the making of art and music and poetry, the fashioning of memory and history and philosophy, the construction of perception and expression and reality

4) an independent publisher with a steadfast goal to print and promote outstanding poets, writers and artists that reflect the creative drive and spirit of the new electronic landscape

NeoPoiesisPress.com

www.ingramcontent.com/pod-product-compliance
Lightning Source LLC
Chambersburg PA
CBHW071712090426
42738CB00009B/1753

« *La création retrouvée* est un ouvrage d'une importance capitale pour le chrétien qui cherche à vivre dans le monde pour la gloire de Dieu, tout en sachant qu'il n'est pas du monde. Albert Wolters trace habilement les contours de la vision chrétienne du monde d'une manière qui ne peut laisser le lecteur indifférent face à ses responsabilités culturelles en tant que créature de Dieu. Je souhaite que ce livre aide à réformer la pensée de plusieurs disciples de Jésus, comme cela a été le cas pour ma pensée, pour mieux comprendre le plan de Dieu pour ce monde meurtri. Qu'il puisse tous nous pousser à être les agents de rédemption que Dieu nous appelle à devenir par la puissance de son Esprit. »

– ALEX FARLEY, professeur d'apologétique, Séminaire Baptiste Évangélique du Québec

« Ce livre est fondamental, car il met en évidence les bases bibliques d'une vision chrétienne du monde. Son auteur est particulièrement qualifié pour expliquer comment le thème *création-chute-rédemption* est la pierre angulaire sur laquelle reposent notre foi et notre vie. »

– WILLIAM EDGAR, professeur d'apologétique, Westminster Theological Seminary

« À la fois court, clair et profondément ancré dans la Parole de Dieu, ce résumé de la vision biblique de la création, de la chute et de la rédemption est l'une des meilleures présentations actuelles sur le sujet. Cet ouvrage encouragera tout chrétien à vivre pleinement sa foi dans le monde que Dieu a créé, et qu'il conduit à sa restauration glorieuse. »

– YANNICK IMBERT, professeur d'apologétique et d'histoire de l'Église, Faculté Jean Calvin